my Book 4

Authors and Advisors

Alma Flor Ada • Kylene Beers • F. Isabel Campoy

Joyce Armstrong Carroll • Nathan Clemens

Anne Cunningham • Martha C. Hougen

Elena Izquierdo • Carol Jago • Erik Palmer

Robert E. Probst • Shane Templeton • Julie Washington

Contributing Consultants

David Dockterman • Mindset Works®

Jill Eggleton

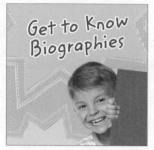

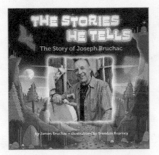
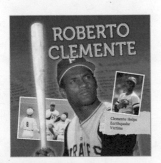

Everyone Has a Story

"He who is not courageous enough to take risks will accomplish nothing in life."

—Muhammad Ali

How do our experiences shape our lives?

Get Curious
Video

Words About Important People

Complete the Vocabulary Network to show what you know
about the words.

account

Meaning: An **account** is a report of something that happened.

Synonyms and Antonyms	Drawing

achieve

Meaning: When you **achieve** something, you get it after a lot of hard work.

Synonyms and Antonyms	Drawing

hurdle

Meaning: A **hurdle** is a problem that could stop you from doing something.

Synonyms and Antonyms	Drawing

Get to Know Biographies

Biographies are a type of informational text. They tell about real people's lives.

Alex wrote his opinion about biographies to share with his class.

Alex Lewis
2nd Grade

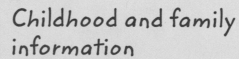

The Elements of a Biography

- ☑ Important dates and events
- ☑ Place of birth
- ☑ Childhood and family information
- ☑ Problems or challenges
- ☑ Why the person is important

Why I Like Reading Biographies

by Alex Lewis

I think biographies are the best kind of book. You can learn so much from them! I like to read them to learn about real people and about history.

I read a biography about the pilot Amelia Earhart. I learned how much she did in her life! She bought her first airplane only a few months after her first flying lesson. In 1932, she became the first woman to fly by herself across the Atlantic Ocean.

I like that biographies can teach us so many different things. I learned about civil rights when I read about Dr. Martin Luther King, Jr. I read about the ways Dr. King helped people get the same rights.

As you can tell, I love biographies. If you like learning about real people and history, read some biographies. I think you'll be a fan of them, too!

Prepare to Read

GENRE STUDY **Biographies** tell about real people's lives. As you read *I Am Helen Keller*, look for:

- events in order from earliest to latest
- information about why this person is important
- ways the person has made a difference

SET A PURPOSE Read to find out the most important ideas in each part. Then **synthesize,** or put together these ideas in your mind, to find out what the text really means to you.

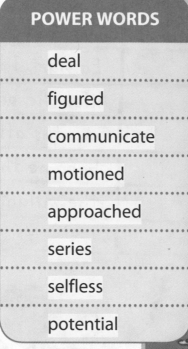

Meet Brad Meltzer.

14

I Am
Helen Keller

by Brad Meltzer

illustrated by Christopher Eliopoulos

I am **Helen Keller**.

When I was little, I was just like you.
I loved to play.
I loved my dog.
And I loved seeing all the bright beautiful flowers.
I also loved copying people. At six months old,
I could already say . . .

On the day I turned one, I started walking.
Oh, and there was another word I always loved.

WAH-WAH.

HERE'S YOUR WATER.

Just like any other kid, right?
But there's one thing that made me different.
When I was nineteen months old, I got very sick.
The doctors said I wouldn't live.
I did live, but the sickness made me blind and deaf.

This is how I see the world.

Close your eyes and block your ears.
I couldn't see anything.
Or hear anything.

That's right.
Nothing.

I know it seems scary.

It was scary for me too.

Back then, people didn't know how to deal with someone who was deaf and blind.

My relatives thought I was a monster.

They were right: I wasn't well-behaved. I was extremely frustrated.

In my dark world, I couldn't tell if anyone noticed me or cared about me.

I couldn't see or hear what I was doing.

But by the time I was five, I'd figured out small ways to communicate.
To say YES, I nodded my head.
For NO, I shook it from side to side.

To say FATHER, I motioned
to put on his glasses.

For MOTHER, I rested
my hand on my face.

For baby sister,
I did this. . .

And when I'd shiver like I
was cold, it really meant. . .

But even with those signs, I couldn't get my dog, Belle, to play with me.
I didn't know how to speak, so I couldn't call her.

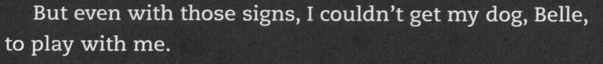

I just wanted to play with my dog.
The saddest part was, I got used to a dark and silent world.

People told my parents to give up on me. That I'd never be good at anything.

They didn't listen, though.

After reading about another blind and deaf girl, my parents found something they hadn't had since I'd gotten sick.

Hope.

We *all* do.

Everyone needs a teacher.

Still, I had no idea what the world was about to bring me.

I never had a more important day.

I was six years old.

From the way my mother was hurrying, I knew something big was coming.

I stood on the porch, waiting, feeling the sun on my face.

Someone approached—I could feel footsteps.

I reached out, thinking it was my mother.

She pulled me into her arms.

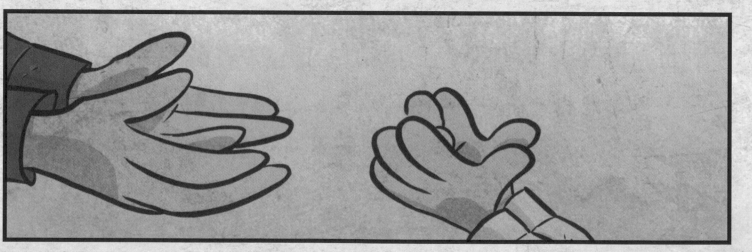

Her name was
Anne Sullivan.
She's the teacher
who changed my life.

In one of her first lessons, she gave me a toy doll.
   After letting me play with it, she spelled the word DOLL into the palm of my hand.

I could feel them.
But I didn't know what letters or words were. Or how they worked.

It didn't stop Miss Sullivan.

One day, we were arguing as she was trying to teach me the words MUG and WATER.

I got so upset, I took my new doll and smashed it on the ground.

I got angry a lot back then.

It was so hard for me.

I was frustrated.

27

Never losing her patience, my teacher took me outside.
At a nearby spout, she put my hand under the
running water.
In my other hand, she spelled the word.
W-A-T-E-R.

W-A-T-E-R.

From there, I realized that everything had a name.
Every object I touched seemed to burst to life.

And now, when I wrote words in my teacher's hand,
I had someone who could understand me.

When you're learning something new, it's often hard.
I started with words.
My vocabulary grew fast.
Eventually, I learned the meaning of the word LOVE.
I had given my teacher some flowers. So she spelled into my hand . . .

Confused, I asked her . . .

"It is here," she spelled while tapping at my heart.
I was still confused.
It was hard to understand something I couldn't touch.

It made no sense. Why couldn't my teacher show me love? But then, she explained . . .

YOU CAN'T TOUCH CLOUDS, BUT YOU CAN FEEL RAIN AND KNOW HOW HAPPY FLOWERS ARE TO GET WATERED.

THAT IS HOW LOVE IS.

YOU CAN'T TOUCH LOVE, BUT YOU CAN FEEL HOW HAPPY IT MAKES YOU.

There, in that moment, my whole world changed.
It was as if there were invisible lines that stretched between me and everyone else in my life.
Close your eyes.
You can feel it too—your connection to your family and friends.

32

Still, life was never easy.

Without sight, I couldn't see people's faces.

Without sound, I couldn't hear their voices.

But one of my greatest breakthroughs came when I learned to do what you're doing right now.

Reading.

To practice, I'd match each word with its object and make sentences.

This was my favorite game.

We played it for hours.

See if you can find the sentence: Girl is in wardrobe.

From there, I started reading real books.
Just like you.

The only difference was, my books were in Braille, which is a series of raised dots that you read with your fingers.

These dots spell my name. H-E-L-E-N.

Want to read *your* name in Braille? Here's the alphabet.

A	B	C	D	E	F
G	H	I	J	K	L
M	N	O	P	Q	R
S	T	U	V	W	X
Y	Z

To make reading even more fun, my teacher took me outside.

She knew I loved feeling the sun on my face and smelling the pine needles.

I read my books so many times, I wore down the raised dots.

There were *The Arabian Nights*, *Robinson Crusoe*, and one of my favorites, *Little Women*.

In those pages, I met brave boys and girls who could hear and see.

"I AM NOT AFRAID OF STORMS, FOR I AM LEARNING HOW TO SAIL MY SHIP."

One of Miss Sullivan's best lessons came when she showed how plants grow.

FEEL THESE BUDS.

SOME BUDS OPEN FAST.

OTHERS OPEN SLOWLY.

A FLOWER CAN ONLY BLOOM IF IT'S WATERED.

When I was nine years old, I wanted to learn how to speak. Even Miss Sullivan was worried about teaching me. She thought I'd get frustrated. But nothing would stop me now.

To help me, Miss Sullivan took me to a teacher named Sarah Fuller, who would put my hand to her face and let me feel her tongue and lips as she made each sound.

In an hour, I learned the letters M, P, A, S, T and I.

Now I could call my dog, and she'd come to me.

At my seventh lesson, I spoke this sentence, the one sentence that I'd repeat over and over:

As I got older, I didn't just learn to speak English. I learned French and German.

For college, I wanted to go to Radcliffe, at Harvard University.

At Harvard, most of my books weren't available in Braille, so Miss Sullivan spelled out many of the textbooks in my hand. That's how much I loved learning. And that's how patient and selfless Miss Sullivan was.

I became the first deaf and blind person to earn a college degree.
I wouldn't be the last.
As I grew older, I wrote twelve books and visited thirty-four countries.
But the most important thing I did was to make sure that other
people with disabilities could get the same education I had.

In my life, they said I was different. They said I'd never be normal. But the truth is, there's no such thing as a "normal" life.

Every one of us is like a flower that must be watered. Every one of us is full of potential.

And every one of us can overcome obstacles.

Look at me.
Hear my words.
I may not be able to see, but I have vision.
I may not be able to hear, but I have a voice.

Think of your life as a hill that must be climbed.

There's no correct path to get to the top.

We all zigzag in our own ways.

At some point, you'll slip,

you'll fall,

you'll tumble back down again.

But if you get back up and keep climbing, I promise you . . .

You will reach the top.

Don't let anything hold you back.
Our lives are what we make of them.
There will always be obstacles.
But there will always be ways around them.

I am Helen Keller
and I won't let anything stop me.

Turn and Talk

Use details from *I Am Helen Keller* to answer these questions with a partner.

1. **Synthesize** Why do you think Helen Keller's life still inspires people today?

2. Who is telling the story? Why do you think the author chose to write the text this way?

3. Why is learning to spell *water* a very important event in Helen's life?

Talking Tip

Be polite. Wait for your turn to talk. Then tell your idea to your partner.

I think that _____.

Write a Life Lesson

PROMPT What is the most important life lesson you learned from *I Am Helen Keller*? How can that lesson be helpful to you and to others? Use details from the text and pictures to explain your ideas.

PLAN First, write the life lesson in the top of the chart. Then, write three reasons why you think the lesson is important.

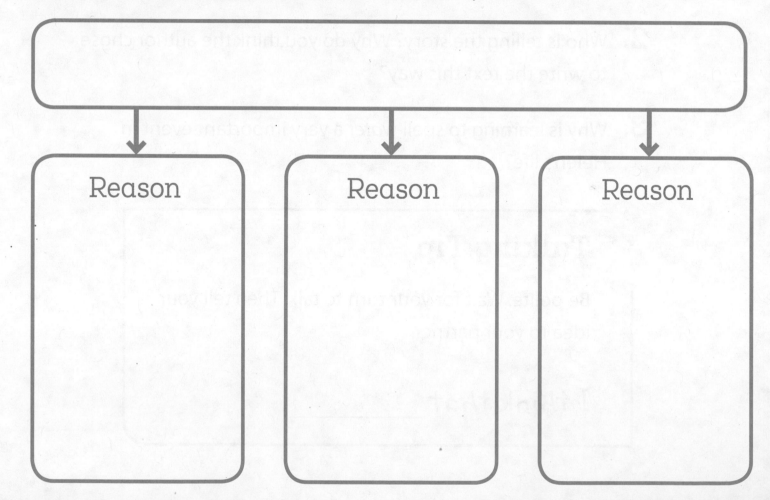

Reason   Reason   Reason

WRITE Now write sentences that describe the life lesson you learned. Explain why you think that lesson can be helpful to you and to others. Remember to:

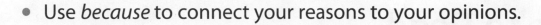

- Use *because* to connect your reasons to your opinions.

- Use language that shows your feelings about the lesson.

_____

_____

_____

_____

_____

_____

_____

_____

_____

_____

_____

Prepare to Read

GENRE STUDY **Biographies** tell about real people's lives.

MAKE A PREDICTION Preview "Aim for the Stars." Franklin Chang-Diaz worked hard to make his dream come true. What do you think his dream was?

_____

_____

_____

_____

_____

_____

_____

SET A PURPOSE Read to find out why Franklin Chang-Diaz is an important person in history.

Aim for the Stars

READ What is Franklin's dream? <u>Underline</u> it.

The Boy from Costa Rica

Franklin Chang-Diaz was the first Hispanic-American astronaut. He was born in 1950 in Costa Rica. His dream was to become an astronaut. To do that, he had to make a big change—move to the United States.

In 1968, Chang-Diaz left his homeland to live in the United States. It was hard for him. He was far from home. He spoke only Spanish. However, he worked hard and did well in school. His dream was about to come true. ▶

> **Close Reading Tip**
>
> Number the main events in order.

READ What does the author want you to think or feel?

☀

Close Reading Tip

Underline the heading.

Living the Dream

Franklin Chang-Diaz joined the U.S. space program in 1980. He became an astronaut in 1981. He went on seven space missions and spent more than 1,600 hours in space! He worked alongside astronauts from many countries. He felt proud to be a part of this community.

Chang-Diaz is not an astronaut anymore, but he is still a scientist. He is working on building a rocket that could make space travel as easy as taking a plane. Imagine that! Franklin Chang-Diaz never met a challenge he could not handle.

CHECK MY UNDERSTANDING

Why did the author call this section "Living the Dream"?

_____

_____

_____

_____

WRITE ABOUT IT Why is it important to learn about Franklin
Chang-Diaz? What does his story teach others? Use details from
the text in your answer.

_____

_____

_____

_____

_____

_____

_____

_____

_____

_____

_____

Prepare to Read

GENRE STUDY **Procedural texts** tell readers how to do or make something. When you read *How to Make a Timeline*, notice:

- directions for readers to follow
- a list of materials needed for the project
- the model, or picture of what the final project will look like
- steps that show order

SET A PURPOSE As you read, stop and think if you don't understand something. Reread, ask yourself questions, use what you already know, and look for visual clues to help you understand the text.

POWER WORDS

timeline

statements

arrange

current

Build Background: Parts of a Timeline

How to Make a

TIMELINE

by Boyd N. Gillin

BIOGRAPHY

A biography tells about the events in a real person's life. It takes time to read a full biography because it has many details and is full of stories.

🕐🕐🕐🕐🕐 **A biography takes time to read.**

THE LIFE OF JOHN HANCOCK

1737	1754	1775
January 23: Born in Braintree, Massachusetts	Graduated from Harvard College	**May 24:** Became president of Congress

TIMELINE

Another way to share information about a person's life is through a timeline. A timeline uses visuals and dates to show a sequence of events at a glance. Because of this, a timeline doesn't have a lot of words on it. You read a timeline from left to right, just like a sentence.

Anyone can make a timeline! A person doesn't have to be famous or a grown-up. Everyone's life is filled with special events.

A timeline gives a lot of information with just a quick glance.

1776

July 4: First person to sign Declaration of Independence

1780

Elected Governor of Massachusetts

Tramayne's TIMELINE

Tramayne made a timeline of his life. Read the statements he wrote. What ideas can you get from Tramayne's timeline to make one about your own life?

To make a timeline about *your* life, think about events from the past that are special to you.

Feb. 13, 2012

Born in
Dallas, Texas

2016

Became a
big brother

Spring 2018

Received an
award from
the library

For example, when were you born? What exciting things have happened to you? Have you won an award or learned a new skill? Write down the dates of important events in your life. If you need help thinking of events or dates, ask family members. You might even learn more about yourself! Let's get started!

Summer 2018

Started taking photography class

Oct. 25, 2018

Started taking trumpet lessons

2019

Helped to plant a tree

CREATE YOUR OWN!

Look back at Tramayne's timeline. Use it as a model to create your own.

Materials

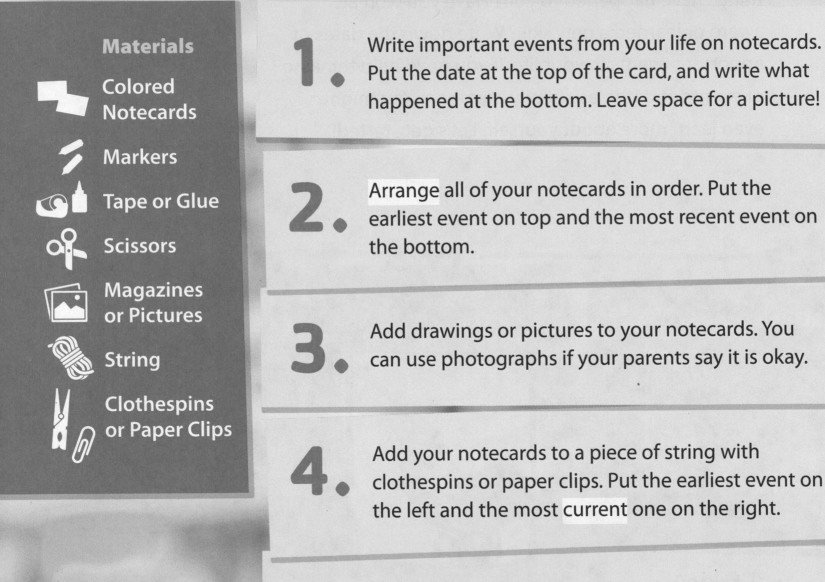

- Colored Notecards
- Markers
- Tape or Glue
- Scissors
- Magazines or Pictures
- String
- Clothespins or Paper Clips

1. Write important events from your life on notecards. Put the date at the top of the card, and write what happened at the bottom. Leave space for a picture!

2. Arrange all of your notecards in order. Put the earliest event on top and the most recent event on the bottom.

3. Add drawings or pictures to your notecards. You can use photographs if your parents say it is okay.

4. Add your notecards to a piece of string with clothespins or paper clips. Put the earliest event on the left and the most current one on the right.

5. Share your timeline with the class. It will be fun to tell your friends about yourself.

Use details from *How to Make a Timeline* to answer these questions with a partner.

1. **Monitor and Clarify** What did you do when you came to a part of the text that you didn't understand? Tell how it helped or didn't help you.

2. Why did the author number the steps on page 56?

3. How do the headings and symbols help you to find and understand information in this text?

Listening Tip

Look at your partner. Listen politely and find out what your partner is saying.

Write an Explanation

PROMPT Choose one event from your timeline. What makes this memory special to you? Explain why it belongs on a timeline about you.

PLAN First, explain why this memory is special to you.

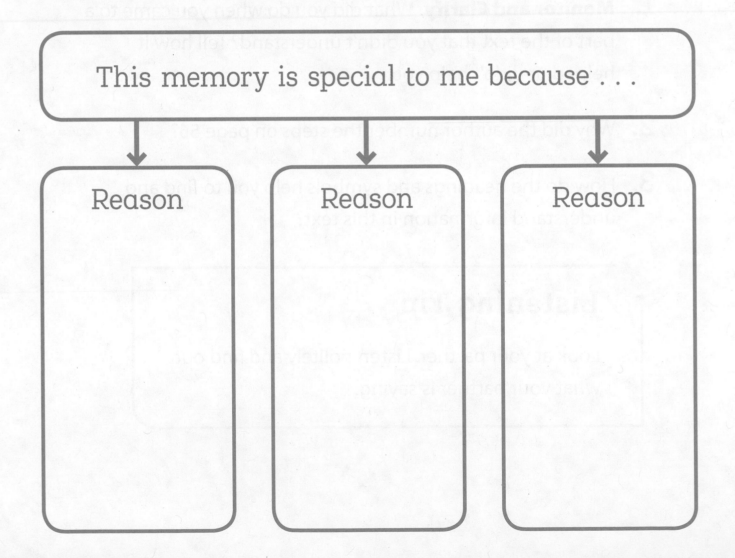

This memory is special to me because . . .

Reason

Reason

Reason

WRITE Now write an explanation to tell why you chose this event for your timeline. Describe why it is important to you. Remember to:

- Include details that tell what you did and how you felt.

- Use details from *How to Make a Timeline* to explain why this event belongs on your timeline.

_____

_____

_____

_____

_____

_____

_____

_____

_____

Prepare to Read

GENRE STUDY **Procedural texts** tell readers how to do or make something.

MAKE A PREDICTION Preview "Make a Me Map!" Think about what procedural texts are like. What do you think you will read about?

_____

_____

_____

_____

_____

_____

SET A PURPOSE Read to learn what a Me Map is and to see if your prediction is right. If not, use what you know about procedural texts to make a new prediction.

my bike

Scooter

James

reading

my friend Lucas

Make a Me Map!

READ How does the picture help you understand how to make a Me Map?

A Me Map is not like other maps. A Me Map is a map of YOU. It tells about who you are and what is important to you. Follow the steps to make a Me Map:

1. First, draw a picture of yourself in the center of a blank sheet of paper using crayons, colored pencils, or markers. Write your name below your picture. ▶

Close Reading Tip

Put a **?** by the parts you have questions about.

CHECK MY UNDERSTANDING

What did you do when you came to a part you didn't understand?

_____

_____

_____

61

READ What is the author's purpose for writing this text?

Close Reading Tip

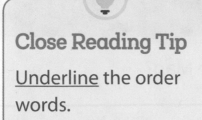

<u>Underline</u> the order words.

2. Next, think about things that are important to you. Ask yourself questions like these to get ideas: *What activities do I like to do? What is my favorite book, food, or color?*

3. Now draw pictures of those things on your map. Then write labels for each picture. For example, if you like to run, you might draw a picture of sneakers and write the word *running* underneath your drawing.

4. Finally, draw lines to connect each of these pictures to the drawing of you in the center.

Now you have your very own Me Map!

CHECK MY UNDERSTANDING

Why does the author include a numbered list? Why is following the steps in order important?

_____

_____

_____

_____

DRAW IT Make a Me Map! Follow the directions in the text to make your own Me Map below. Look carefully at the picture of James's Me Map to help you think of ideas.

Prepare to Read

GENRE STUDY **Biographies** tell about real people's lives. As you read *The Stories He Tells: The Story of Joseph Bruchac,* notice:

- details and events in the person's life
- events in order from earliest to latest
- photos of the person

SET A PURPOSE Read to make smart guesses, or **inferences,** about things the author does not say. Use clues in the text and pictures to help you.

POWER WORDS

ashamed

elders

overflowing

pride

Meet
James Bruchac.

THE STORIES HE TELLS

The Story of Joseph Bruchac

by James Bruchac • illustrations by Brendan Kearney

Joseph Bruchac III was born on October 16, 1942. He was born in Saratoga Springs, New York. His parents' names were Joseph Jr. and Marion Flora Bowman. Joseph grew up in Greenfield Center, New York. That is in the foothills of the Adirondack Mountains.

Joseph in second grade

Joseph was raised by his mother's parents. His grandfather was an Abenaki Indian. He had a strong love for animals and nature. His grandmother was one of the first women to ever graduate from Albany Law School. She liked books and learning.

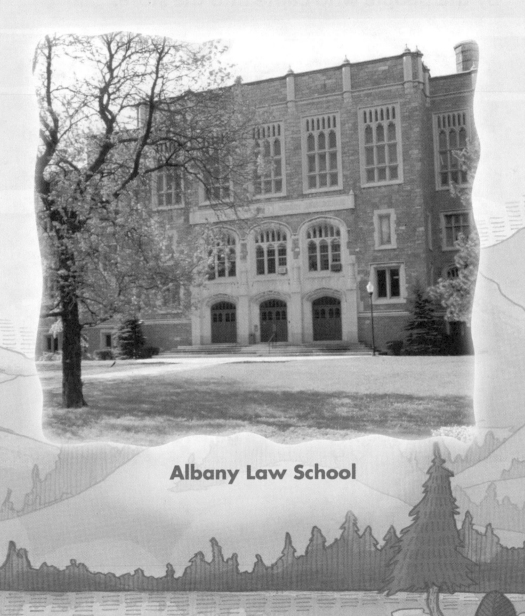

Albany Law School

Joseph's grandparents ran a small general store and gas station right next to the house where he grew up. The store was on one of the main roads into the Adirondack Mountains. As a boy, Joseph loved to hear all of the stories and tall tales told by the people who came into the store.

Joseph's family's general store

There were not many children out in the country where Joseph lived. Because of this, he often played by himself in the forest. Sometimes he would walk by Grandpa Jesse's side. Grandpa Jesse taught Joseph a lot about animals, nature, and gardening. He never spoke much about his Native American background. Grandpa Jesse and his family and other Native Americans had been treated badly.

Joseph and his grandfather

Grandpa Jesse said he left school when he was in fourth grade. Why? He was being called mean names. Hearing such family stories made Joseph feel sad. It also made him want to learn more. He wanted to learn the stories and traditions his grandfather was too **ashamed** to share.

Joseph's grandmother passed on to him a love of school. With this, Joseph went to college at Cornell University. While in college, he began to learn everything he could learn about Native American ways and beliefs. As an adult, Joseph traveled the country meeting Native American **elders**. These elders gladly shared their stories and traditions with him.

Cornell University

Joseph and his wife Carol met in college. They married and had two sons named James and Jesse. Joseph was **overflowing** with stories that he would often retell to his two sons.

Before long, Joseph began to share the stories with others outside the family. Times had changed a lot since Grandpa Jesse left school. Now when Joseph told the stories, people listened and were interested. They felt Joseph's retellings were important. They respected him. Joseph also began to write stories in books.

Joseph sharing stories

In just a few years, Joseph Bruchac became known all across the world as a Native American storyteller. He has won many awards for his storytelling. Joseph has also written more than 120 books of poetry, fiction, and nonfiction. Most of the books are about Native Americans.

Joseph connects with audiences around the world.

Growing up learning about Native American traditions, James and Jesse are also storytellers. Joseph's oldest son, James, is also a wilderness and tracking expert. His younger son, Jesse, teaches the Abenaki language.

James at work

Jesse, James, and Joseph Bruchac

Joseph still lives in the house where he grew up. He writes and shares stories almost every day. He takes extra pride in seeing a love for stories continue to his grandkids. He and his sons continue to help pass along these once hidden traditions to future generations!

Joseph and his grandchildren

Use details from *The Stories He Tells: The Story of Joseph Bruchac* to answer these questions with a partner.

1. **Make Inferences** Why is passing on traditions important to Joseph Bruchac? Use evidence from the text to explain your answer.

2. Why did the author write this text?

3. Think about what the text and photos tell you about Joseph Bruchac. What qualities do you think a person needs to be a great storyteller?

Listening Tip

Listen carefully to your partner. Think of what you agree with and do not agree with.

75

Write a Letter

PROMPT What would you say in a letter to Joseph Bruchac?
What questions would you ask him? Think about which details in
the text were most interesting to you and made you curious.

PLAN First, list interesting facts you learned about Mr. Bruchac.
Then write questions you would like to ask him.

Facts	My Questions

WRITE Now write a letter to Joseph Bruchac. Ask him questions about his life and work. Tell which fact about his life is most interesting to you. Explain why. Remember to:

- Use commas in your greeting and closing.

- Begin your questions with *what, why, who, when,* or *how.*

_____

_____

_____

_____

_____

_____

_____

_____

_____

_____

_____

Prepare to Read

GENRE STUDY **Biographies** tell about real people's lives.

MAKE A PREDICTION Preview "A Way with Animals."

Temple Grandin knows a lot about how animals behave. You know that biographies tell about events in a person's life in order. What do you think you will learn about Temple Grandin?

_____

_____

_____

_____

_____

_____

SET A PURPOSE Read to find out what makes Temple Grandin an animal expert.

A Way with Animals

Temple Grandin is a scientist and animal expert. She was born in 1947 in Massachusetts. She did not have an easy childhood. Temple has autism. People with autism sometimes have trouble speaking and learning. Going to school was challenging for her. Some teachers did not understand how to help her learn.

When she was in high school, Temple spent a summer at her aunt's cattle farm. She noticed that being around the cows made her feel better. ▶

Close Reading Tip

Put a ? by the parts you have questions about.

READ How does Temple use her special gift? <u>Underline</u> the sentences that tell you.

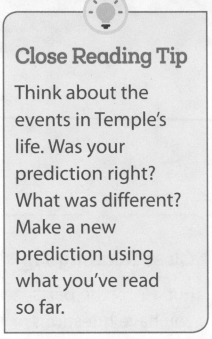

Close Reading Tip

Think about the events in Temple's life. Was your prediction right? What was different? Make a new prediction using what you've read so far.

Temple Grandin discovered that she had a way with animals. She understood them and how their minds worked. Temple decided to use her special gifts to teach people about animals. She decided to make it her life's work.

Today, Temple travels around the country and speaks about how to take good care of animals. She speaks about autism, too. Her accomplishments have made her a hero and an inspiration to others.

CHECK MY UNDERSTANDING

What is the central idea of this text?

_____

_____

_____

_____

_____

WRITE ABOUT IT Temple Grandin believes that animals have helped her as much as she has helped them. Which details in the text support this idea?

_____

_____

_____

_____

_____

_____

_____

_____

_____

_____

_____

Prepare to Read

GENRE STUDY **Poetry** uses images, sounds, and rhythm to express feelings. As you read *Drum Dream Girl,* look for:

- words that appeal to the senses
- words that make you think of powerful images or pictures
- words that describe

SET A PURPOSE As you read, **create mental images,** or make pictures in your mind, to help you understand details in the text.

POWER WORDS

secret

whir

reminding

dared

alone

deserved

starlit

allowed

Meet Margarita Engle.

DRUM DREAM GIRL

by Margarita Engle

illustrated by

Rafael López

On an island of music
in a city of drumbeats
the drum dream girl
dreamed

of pounding tall conga drums

tapping small *bongó* drums

and boom boom booming

with long, loud sticks

on big, round, silvery

moon-bright *timbales.*

But everyone

on the island of music

in the city of drumbeats

believed that only boys

should play drums

so the drum dream girl

had to keep dreaming

quiet

secret

drumbeat

dreams.

At outdoor cafés that looked like gardens

she heard drums played by men

but when she closed her eyes

she could also hear

her own imaginary

music.

When she walked under
wind-wavy palm trees
in a flower-bright park
she heard the whir of parrot wings
the clack of woodpecker beaks
the dancing tap
of her own footsteps
and the comforting pat
of her own
heartbeat.

91

At carnivals, she listened
to the rattling beat
of towering
dancers
on stilts

and the dragon clang
of costumed drummers
wearing huge masks.

At home, her fingertips
rolled out their own
dreamy drum rhythm
on tables and chairs . . .

and even though everyone
kept reminding her that girls
on the island of music
had never played drums

95

the brave drum dream girl

dared to play

tall conga drums

small *bongó* drums

and big, round, silvery

moon-bright *timbales*.

Her hands seemed to fly

as they rippled

rapped

and pounded

all the rhythms

of her drum dreams.

Her big sisters were so excited

that they invited her to join

their new all-girl dance band

but their father said only boys

should play drums.

So the drum dream girl

had to keep dreaming

and drumming

alone

until finally
her father offered
to find a music teacher
who could decide if her drums
deserved
to be heard.

The drum dream girl's
teacher was amazed.
The girl knew so much
but he taught her more
and more
and more

and she practiced
and she practiced
and she practiced

until the teacher agreed

that she was ready

to play her small *bongó* drums

outdoors at a starlit café

that looked like a garden

where everyone who heard

her dream-bright music

sang

and danced

and decided

that girls should always

be allowed to play

drums

and both girls and boys

should feel free

to dream.

Use details from *Drum Dream Girl* to answer these questions with a partner.

1. **Create Mental Images** What does the drum dream girl dream about? Which of the poem's words help you picture it in your mind?

2. What does the drum dream girl do when her father says only boys play drums? What does that tell you about her?

3. What is the poet's message?

Talking Tip

Answer your partner's questions. Explain your ideas clearly.

I mean that _____.

Write a Journal Entry

PROMPT How would the drum dream girl describe her first concert at the starlit café? What did she see, hear, and feel? Use details from the text and illustrations to explain your answer.

PLAN First, fill in the web with four details about the concert.

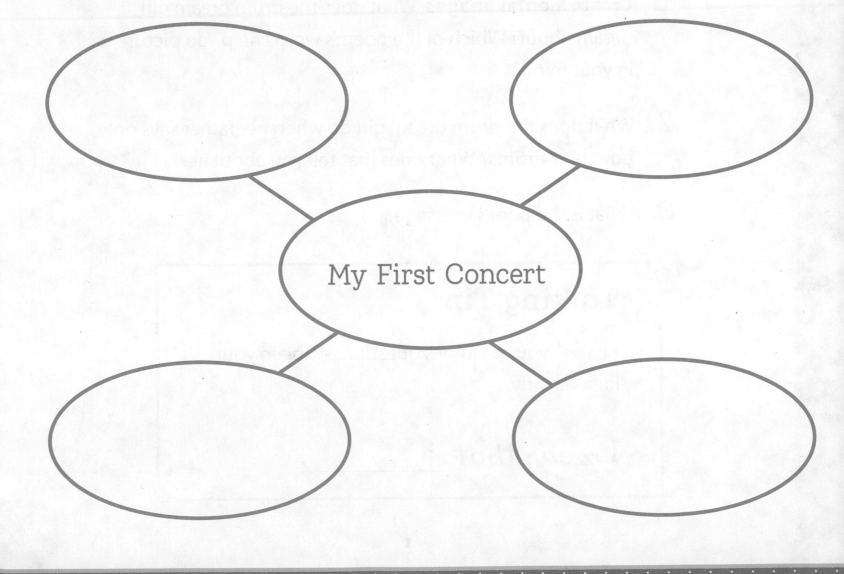

My First Concert

WRITE Now write a journal entry from the drum dream girl's point of view that describes the night of the concert. Remember to:

- Use what you know about the drum dream girl to explain how she feels that night.

- Use the words *I* and *me* to tell the story as she would.

_____

_____

_____

_____

_____

_____

_____

_____

_____

_____

Prepare to Read

GENRE STUDY **Poetry** uses images, sounds, and rhythm to express feelings.

MAKE A PREDICTION Preview "A Dancer's Journey." This poem is about a famous ballerina. What do you think you will learn about her?

_____

_____

_____

_____

_____

_____

_____

SET A PURPOSE Read to find out about the life of Maria Tallchief.

A Dancer's Journey

READ What do you picture in your mind as you read?

Maria Tallchief was a Native American ballerina. She was born in 1925 in Oklahoma. This poem is about her life:

Picture yourself in Oklahoma

Where the plains stretch on and the wind blows free.

Music is playing and a child is dancing

It must be young Betty Marie! ▶

> **Close Reading Tip**
> Underline words that help you picture the setting.

CHECK MY UNDERSTANDING

What do you know about Maria Tallchief as a child?

_____

_____

READ How does the photo help you understand the poem?

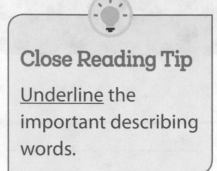

Close Reading Tip

<u>Underline</u> the important describing words.

Picture yourself in California

Where bridges sparkle and sea meets sky.

A young ballerina amazes the crowd.

"Maria!" the people cry.

Picture yourself in New York City

Where people are waiting to see a ballet.

The curtain rises and the crowd holds its breath—

Tallchief is performing today!

CHECK MY UNDERSTANDING

What do you picture in your mind when you read this part of the poem?

_____

_____

_____

110

WRITE ABOUT IT Think about the different settings in "A Dancer's Journey." Why do you think the poet chose to use more than one setting? Use details from the poem in your answer.

_____

_____

_____

_____

_____

_____

_____

_____

_____

_____

_____

Prepare to View

GENRE STUDY **Videos** are short movies that give you information or something for you to watch for enjoyment. As you watch *Roberto Clemente,* notice:

- how pictures, sounds, and words work together
- what the video is about
- how the video makes you feel
- the tone or mood of the video

SET A PURPOSE When others want to persuade you to agree with an idea, they give reasons to support it. Pay attention to the ideas and opinions in the video. Listen for facts and reasons that support them. What does the narrator want you to think or believe about Roberto Clemente?

Build Background: Baseball

ROBERTO CLEMENTE

Clemente Helps
Earthquake
Victims

As You View As you watch the video, listen to the words carefully. Look for evidence that shows what type of person Roberto Clemente was. Think about whether the video is trying to make you think or feel a certain way.

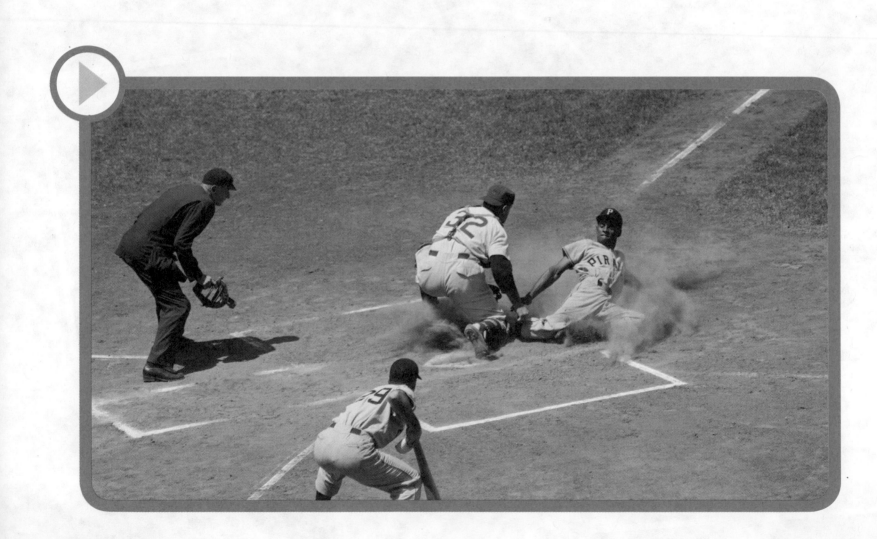

Use details from *Roberto Clemente* to answer these questions with a partner.

1. **Ideas and Support** The narrator says that Roberto Clemente was a kind, caring man. Which details in the video support that opinion?

2. In your own words, describe the important events in Roberto Clemente's life in the order they happened.

3. What is the central idea of the video? What does the narrator want you to think and feel?

Talking Tip

Wait for your turn to speak. Tell about your feelings and ideas clearly.

I feel that _____.

Let's Wrap Up!

(?) Essential Question

How do our experiences shape our lives?

Pick one of these activities to show what you have learned about the topic.

1. Biographies Rule!

Think about the texts you have read. What makes a great biography? Using details from the texts, write six rules a writer should follow to write a great biography.

Word Challenge

Can you use the word achieve in your rules?

2. Show a Lesson

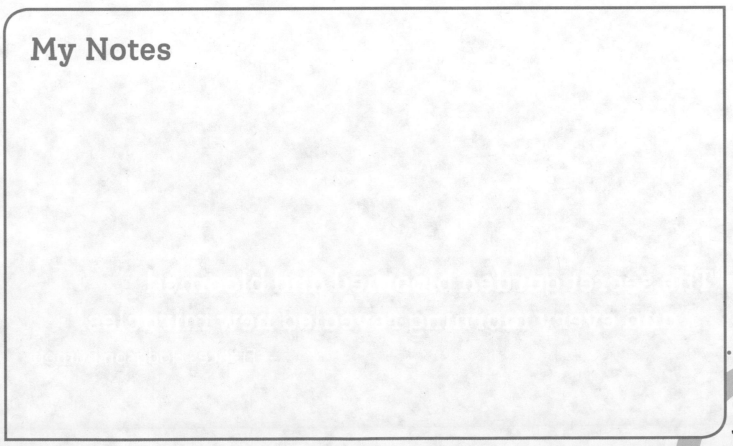

Create a poster that shares a life lesson you learned from one of the texts. Think about how words, colors, designs, or pictures can grab someone's attention and make him or her think. Share your poster with a group. Explain why you think that lesson is important.

My Notes

Time to Grow!

"The secret garden bloomed and bloomed
and every morning revealed new miracles."

—Frances Hodgson Burnett

? Essential Question

What do plants need to live and grow?

Get Curious Video

119

Words About Plants

Complete the Vocabulary Network to show what you know about the words.

fertilize	
Meaning: When you **fertilize** soil, you add something that helps plants grow.	
Synonyms and Antonyms	Drawing

germinate

Meaning: Seeds **germinate** when they begin to grow.

Synonyms and Antonyms	Drawing

survive

Meaning: When things **survive**, they stay alive.

Synonyms and Antonyms	Drawing

THE GROWTH OF A SUNFLOWER

A **photo essay** is a group of photographs that tells a story or explains something. The photos may be paired with text, too. Look at the photos and read the captions to learn how a plant grows.

1

Find a large pot with holes in the bottom. Fill the pot with soil and then plant the seed.

2

Cover the seed with soil. Add water and sun.

3

After a few days, the seed germinates, or begins to grow. Give the seedling water and sun. This keeps it growing. You can fertilize it, too.

BLOOM!

5

4

As the bud
opens, the
flower begins
to form.

The young plant grows taller.
Be sure it still gets water and
sunlight. Soon, a bud starts
to develop.

123

Prepare to Read

GENRE STUDY **Informational text** is nonfiction. It gives facts about a topic. As you read *Experiment with What a Plant Needs to Grow*, pay attention to:

- photos with labels
- order of events
- cause and effect
- ways that pictures and words help readers understand the text

SET A PURPOSE Think about the author's words as you read. Then **evaluate,** or decide, which of the details are most important to help you understand the text.

POWER WORDS

- minerals
- fuels
- process
- provides
- sprout
- moisten
- seedlings
- spiky

Meet Nadia Higgins.

Experiment with What a Plant Needs to Grow

by

Nadia Higgins

What Are Plants?

Plants are living things. They grow. They reproduce. Like you, plants need air and water. They need minerals to stay healthy. They also need food.

For a plant, food starts with sunlight. Sunlight fuels photosynthesis. This is a process in which green leaves make food using air and water.

With enough sunlight and water, flowering plants will bloom.

Plants give us food, wood, and medicine. Photosynthesis **provides** the oxygen we need to breathe!

Can Seeds Get Too Much Water?

Water helps a plant stay strong and sturdy. But even before a plant shoots out of the ground, its seeds need water to sprout.

Can seeds get too much water? Let's find out.

Plants die if they don't get enough water.

What you need:

water

three small bowls

six cotton balls

handful of grass seeds

pencil and paper

127

Steps:

1. Start by putting two cotton balls in each of the bowls.

2. Next, fill the first bowl so the cotton balls are covered with water. Moisten the second bowl's cotton balls all the way through. Don't add any water to the third bowl.

3. Sprinkle about a dozen seeds on top of the cotton balls in each bowl.

Label the bowls so you remember which is which.

Very Wet

A little Wet

Dry

Keep checking your **seedlings** for a week. Which sprouts are the tallest and sturdiest?

4. Put the cotton balls in a sunny place.

5. Check the bowls every day. Make sure the first two cotton balls stay covered in water. Make sure the second two stay moist.

After a few days, some seeds will sprout.

Think It Through

A seed has a coat that protects it. Water softens the coat, so the seed can sprout. But seeds also need air. Too much water can keep a seed from getting enough air.

Horse chestnuts have **spiky** seed coats to protect their seeds.

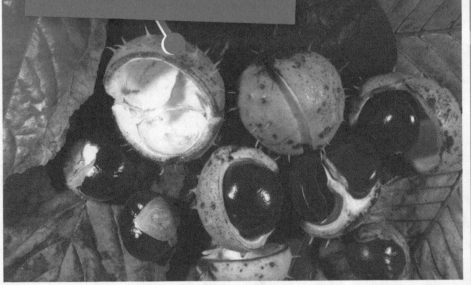

Now Try This

Plants need minerals to be healthy. Most plants get minerals from the soil. Predict how long your grass can survive without soil. Watch the grass sprouts to see if you were right.

Be sure to write down your prediction before you start experimenting.

How Do Leaves Get Air?

We just saw that seeds need air to sprout. Roots need air, too. Air is also part of photosynthesis.

As they make food, green leaves take air in and let it out. Let's find out how.

You can easily poke your finger into good garden soil. The loose soil holds lots of tiny spaces. Those air-filled spaces keep roots healthy.

What you need:

petroleum jelly

leafy green plant

camera

masking tape

Steps:

1. Spread a heavy coat of petroleum jelly over the tops of five leaves of your plant.

2. Do the same on the undersides of five other leaves.

3. Put your plant in a sunny window. Then take its picture..

4. Observe your plant every day for the next week.

Mark the tops of the coated leaves with tape so you can easily find them again.

Compare what you see to the photo you took on the first day.

How are the leaves different from your photo?

Think It Through

Petroleum jelly kept some of the leaves from letting air in and out. Those leaves started to wilt. The leaves that were coated on the bottom wilted the most.

Measure Like a Scientist

Measuring helps scientists show exactly what is happening. Let's look at some ways you might use measuring in a plant experiment.

Measurement	Test	Tool	Unit (metric)
Weight	Weigh two seeds. Is one heavier?	Scale	Ounces (grams)
Length	Measure a bean seedling in the morning. Then measure it the next day. Did it grow taller?	Ruler	Inches (centimeters)
Time	Track how many days it takes for a plant to bloom.	Calendar	Days
Volume	Measure how much water you are adding to a pot.	Measuring cup	Cup (milliliters)

Use details from *Experiment with What a Plant Needs to Grow* to answer these questions with a partner.

1. **Evaluate** What are the most important facts in *Experiment with What a Plant Needs to Grow*? Look for clues in the text and photos to help you decide.

2. How do the captions and labels on pages 128 and 129 help you understand the experiment?

3. Some pages have numbered steps and some do not. Why did the author organize the text this way?

Talking Tip

Ask a question if you are not sure about your partner's ideas.

Why did you say _____?

Write a Lab Report

PROMPT Imagine you are conducting one of the experiments in the text. What observations would you make? What conclusions could you draw? Use details from the text and photos to explain your ideas.

PLAN First, write or draw what you would see at the beginning of the experiment. Next, write or draw what you would see at the end of the experiment.

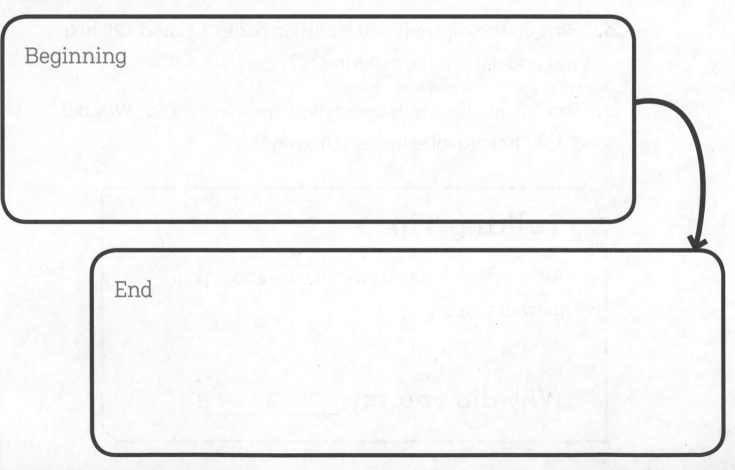

Beginning

End

WRITE Now write three observations you would make during the experiment. Then write a conclusion you can make from your observations. Remember to:

- Use details from the text to describe what you see and do.

- Use words such as *first, then,* and *next* to tell the order of your observations.

_____

_____

_____

_____

_____

_____

_____

_____

_____

_____

Prepare to Read

GENRE STUDY **Informational text** is nonfiction. It gives facts about a topic.

MAKE A PREDICTION Preview "Butterfly Garden." You can grow a garden that butterflies will like to visit. Look carefully at the structure of the text. What do you think you will read about?

_____

_____

_____

_____

_____

_____

_____

SET A PURPOSE Read to learn how to grow a butterfly garden.

Butterfly Garden

READ What is this section mostly about? <u>Underline</u> the sentences that are the most important.

Butterflies are great insects to have in a garden. A pretty flower is even prettier when a butterfly lands on it! Also, butterflies help plants grow. As they visit flowers to drink nectar, they move pollen from flower to flower. Pollen is a yellow dust that comes from flowers. Plants use pollen to make more seeds that grow into plants. ▶

Close Reading Tip

Find an opinion. Mark it with *.

CHECK MY UNDERSTANDING

Why are butterflies nice to have in a garden?

_____

_____

READ What is the author's purpose for writing this text?

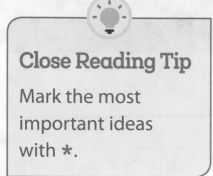

Close Reading Tip

Mark the most important ideas with *.

If you want butterflies to come to your garden, then plant flowers that attract butterflies. Butterflies like brightly colored wildflowers, such as red clovers. Follow these simple steps to grow a garden that butterflies will like to visit.

1. Buy a pack of seeds that says the flowers will attract butterflies.

2. Find a sunny spot and prepare the soil for planting. Remove weeds and break up clumps of dirt.

3. Scatter your seeds in the fine, crumbly dirt. Then use a rake to mix up the seeds and soil.

4. Water your garden regularly. When your flowers bloom, keep an eye out for butterfly visitors!

CHECK MY UNDERSTANDING

What will cause butterflies to come to your garden?

_____

_____

_____

140

WRITE ABOUT IT In your own words, describe how to grow a butterfly garden. Be sure to tell the steps in order.

_____

_____

_____

_____

_____

_____

_____

_____

_____

_____

_____

_____

Prepare to Read

GENRE STUDY **Fairy tales** are old stories that have made-up characters and events that could not happen. As you read *Jack and the Beanstalk,* look for:

- the beginning, middle, and ending of the story
- characters who are not found in real life
- an ending that is happy
- storytelling phrases (*once upon a time, happily ever after*)

SET A PURPOSE As you read, **retell** the story. Use your own words to tell what happens in the beginning, middle, and end of the story.

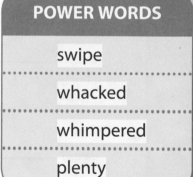

POWER WORDS
swipe
whacked
whimpered
plenty

Meet Helen Lester.

Jack and the Beanstalk

by Helen Lester   illustrated by Jesús Aguado

Once upon a time, a boy named Jack lived with his mother in a poor little hut. What money they had for food came from selling milk from their cow, Moozetta. But when old Moozetta stopped giving milk, they knew they would have to sell *her*. So Jack and the cow hiked into the village. Hours later, Jack returned alone with a handful of beans. *Beans*? Beans.

"You've got to be kidding me!" yelled Jack's mother. "You were supposed to sell Moozetta for MONEY! Beans can't buy food!"

"But the beans are so pretty," said Jack.

"This is a mess," sighed his mother.

Jack went outside and planted the pretty beans in a sunny spot. He gave them a drink of water. Maybe, just maybe, they would grow. And grow they did!

Overnight, the seeds had sprouted. By morning, they had wound into a beautiful beanstalk.

"How did it grow so fast?" wondered Jack.

It had grown up…up…up and out of sight, beyond the clouds.

"WOWEE!" exclaimed Jack. Being a curious lad, he simply had to climb it.

Where would the beanstalk lead? He went up and up, higher and higher, until he went beyond the clouds.

GO AWAY!
ONLY GIANTS
ALLOWED!

BEWARE:
LARGE HUNGRY
BEINGS

Tada! Jack gazed upon an enormous castle.
He saw some creepy-looking signs, too.
From inside the castle a voice boomed,

"Fee-fi-fo-fum!
Time for beddy. Ho-dee-hum."

On the ground was a little bag of gold.

Jack looked left and right, and—SWIPE!—
down the beanstalk he went with his treasure. The
big sleeper surely wouldn't miss such a small bag.
At the sight of the gold, Jack's mother allowed
herself a smile.

The next morning, Jack climbed the beanstalk again.

**"Fee-fi-fo-fum!
Time for beddy. Ho-dee-hum."**

"Good timing," thought Jack, and this time he helped himself to a goose who was very busy laying golden eggs.

At the sight of the busy goose cranking out golden eggs, Jack's mother allowed herself a giggle.

The next morning, Jack eagerly climbed the beanstalk. He wondered what treasures awaited him. Oh, dear. He did not find what he had expected.

"Fee-fi-fo-fum!
WHERE ON EARTH DID YOU COME FROM?"

"From down on Earth," replied Jack. "Well, I came up my beanstalk, which is IN earth. You see, I gave it sunshine, and water, and — "

But the giant was not interested in Jack's gardening skills. He was HUNGRY! Jack, being nimble and quick, hurried down the beanstalk.

As the giant followed and was halfway down, Jack grabbed an ax, whacked the beanstalk, and SPLAT.

"My toe hurts," whimpered the giant. "And how will I get home?"

"I'll show you," said Jack kindly. First, he showed the giant how to water the beanstalk. Together, they cared for the plant. It grew up and up beyond the clouds.

Now the giant could climb home, and Jack bought Moozetta back. He returned everything he had taken from the giant. The gentle giant told his new friends they could keep the goose.

From that day on, Jack, his mother, the goose, and Moozetta had plenty to eat and lived happily ever after.

Once in a while, they invited the giant down for a giant feast. These feasts always included plenty of leafy beanstalk greens.

Use details from *Jack and the Beanstalk* to answer these questions with a partner.

1. **Retell** In your own words, retell the most important story events in order.

2. On page 146, why does the author repeat the words *up* and *higher*? What is she trying to show the reader?

3. How do you think Jack felt when he first saw the giant? How do his feelings change? Use details from the text and pictures to explain your answer.

Listening Tip

Listen carefully and politely. Look at your partner to show you are paying attention.

Write a Dos and Don'ts List

PROMPT If you want to make friends with a giant, what should you do? What shouldn't you do? Use details from *Jack and the Beanstalk* and other stories you've read about giants to explain your answer.

PLAN First, write or draw one thing you *should* do in the "Do" box. Next, write or draw one thing you *should not* do in the "Don't" box.

Do	Don't

WRITE Now write a list of tips to help someone make friends with a giant. Remember to:

- Include tips that tell what to do and what *not* to do.

- Use what you know about giants from *Jack and the Beanstalk* and other stories you have read.

_____

_____

_____

_____

_____

_____

_____

_____

_____

_____

_____

Prepare to Read

GENRE STUDY **Fairy tales** are old stories that have made-up characters and events that could not happen.

MAKE A PREDICTION Preview "The Princess and the Pea." A lonely prince must marry a *real* princess. How do you think he will find the right princess?

_____

_____

_____

_____

_____

_____

SET A PURPOSE Read to find out how the prince will find a *real* princess to marry.

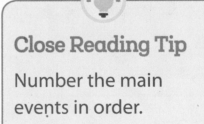

The Princess and the Pea

READ What is the story's problem? <u>Underline</u> it.

Long ago, there was a lonely prince. His parents wanted him to marry a *real* princess. He wanted his wife to be smart and funny, but he couldn't find a princess who was both.

One stormy night, the prince heard a knock on the door. He opened it to find a young woman in wet clothes.

"My silly horse ran home without me!" she said. "I knew that a royal family would help me, for I am a *real* princess." ▶

> **Close Reading Tip**
>
> Number the main events in order.

CHECK MY UNDERSTANDING

What happens at the beginning of the story?

_____

_____

157

READ Why does the queen go to the royal garden? <u>Underline</u> it.

Close Reading Tip

Number the main events in order.

When the queen saw the prince and the young woman laughing, she knew they were falling in love. She made a plan. She went to the royal garden to pick the very smallest pea she could find. Then she placed several mattresses on top of each other and placed the tiny pea under the bottom mattress.

In the morning, the queen asked the princess how she had slept. The princess wanted to be polite, but she always told the truth. She told the queen that an enormous lump in the bed had kept her awake for most of the night. Since only a *real* princess would have felt the tiny pea, the queen told the prince he could marry her. They all lived happily ever after.

CHECK MY UNDERSTANDING

How is the story's problem solved?

_____

_____

_____

WRITE ABOUT IT Imagine you are the prince. Retell "The
Princess and the Pea" from his point of view. Use the words *I, me*,
and *my* to describe the events of the story in order.

_____

_____

_____

_____

_____

_____

_____

_____

_____

_____

Prepare to Read

GENRE STUDY **Fairy tales** are old stories that have made-up characters and events that could not happen. As you read *Jackie and the Beanstalk,* look for:

- clues that the story is make-believe
- an ending that is happy
- how pictures and words help you understand what happens

SET A PURPOSE As you read, **make connections** by finding ways that this text is like things in your life and other texts you have read. This will help you understand and remember the text.

POWER WORDS

adorable

oversized

hauling

glanced

Meet Lori Mortensen.

JACKIE
AND THE
BEANSTALK

by Lori Mortensen
illustrated by Ben Scruton

Once upon a time, a girl named Jackie lived in an apartment with her father.

It was crowded and messy because they lived with a GIGANTIC cow.

What was a cow doing there? Eating, mostly.

It eats like a cow!

Buying the cow had been a stupendously bad idea, but nobody thought of that when it was a cute little calf.

Adorable! Can we buy it?

Sure!

The woman had no money, but she did have some special beans.

Plant them in some dirt, add some water, and wait. By morning, SHAZAM! There'll be a beanstalk stretching up to the sky like a winding green staircase.

Are you sure? Plant growth takes dirt, water, sun, and time!

Jackie looked at the cow and then looked at the beans. Suddenly, pocketing the beans sounded a whole lot better than hauling the cow back home.

Deal!

Of course, when Jackie got home, her father hit the roof. Well, not really, but he did toss the beans out the window and yell a lot.

A few beans for a whole cow?

Overnight, the beans sprouted long, green tendrils that twisted and reached up toward the sky.

The next morning, there it was, exactly as the woman promised—the biggest beanstalk Jackie had ever seen.

Wow! I've never seen a plant grow so fast! I wonder what's at the top. Maybe there's treasure!

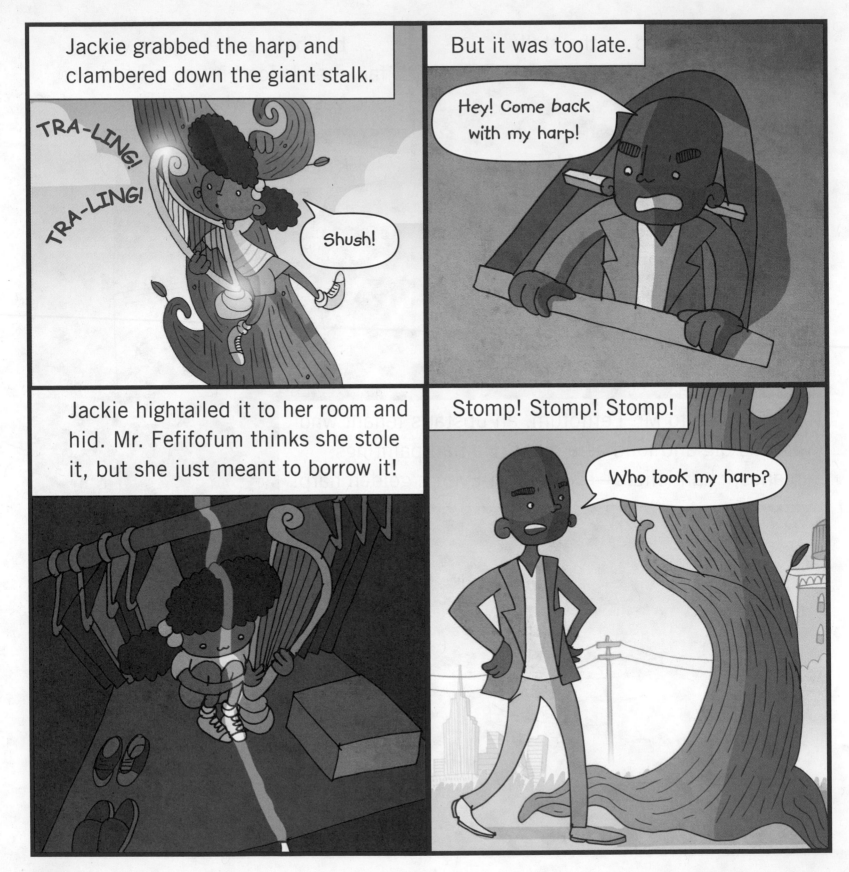

169

Did Jackie ever find treasure? No, but she did start a business that turned into a gigantic success . . .

. . . and lived happily ever after.

Use details from *Jackie and the Beanstalk* to answer these questions with a partner.

1. **Make Connections** How are *Jackie and the Beanstalk* and *Jack and the Beanstalk* alike? How are they different?

2. Why do you think Jackie's father lets her get a cow for a pet? What causes him to change his mind about it?

3. What problem does Jackie have after she climbs the beanstalk? How does she solve it?

Talking Tip

Share your ideas. Speak clearly and not too fast or too slow.

I think that _____.

Write a Story

PROMPT How would the story be different if the cow told it? Think about how the cow's point of view is different from the other characters'. Use details from the words and pictures to explain your ideas.

PLAN First, draw or write what happens first, next, and last in the cow's story.

First

⬇

Next

⬇

Last

WRITE Now write the cow's version of the story. Help your readers get to know the cow! Include details that tell what she is like and how she feels about the story events. Remember to:

- Tell the story events in order.

- Use the words *I* and *me* to write in the cow's voice.

_____

_____

_____

_____

_____

_____

_____

_____

_____

_____

Prepare to Read

GENRE STUDY **Fairy tales** are old stories that have made-up characters and events that could not happen.

MAKE A PREDICTION Preview "The Prince and the Tasty Pea." A princess has a different opinion from her parents about who she should marry. What do you think will happen?

_____

_____

_____

_____

_____

_____

SET A PURPOSE Read to find out how the princess's life changes.

The Prince and the Tasty Pea

READ What is the setting of the story? <u>Underline</u> it.

Once upon a time, a princess lived in a giant castle. Her parents wanted her to marry a prince. She wanted to marry someone who was kind and had lots in common with her.

One rainy night, a kind young man came to the castle. He said he was a prince and asked if he could spend the night. The queen was not sure she believed him. She decided to put a pea under his mattress to find out if he was a *real* prince. ▶

Close Reading Tip

Mark important words with *.

CHECK MY UNDERSTANDING

Why does the queen want to be sure he is a real prince?

_____

_____

175

READ What do you learn about the princess in this section?

Close Reading Tip

Write **C** when you make a connection.

That night, a lump in the bed kept the prince awake. He lifted the mattress and discovered the pea, which he quickly ate. It was so tasty that he went to the garden for more. To his surprise, the princess was gardening. She explained that she loved to garden, but her parents didn't think a princess should do any kind of work. She had to sneak out at night to garden.

The prince and princess talked about soil and seeds, watering and weeds. By morning, they decided to marry and open their own royal garden stand. As soon as the queen heard that the pea had kept the prince awake, she started planning the wedding. And they all lived…well, you know.

CHECK MY UNDERSTANDING

How do you think the princess feels at the end of the story? Use the text and pictures for clues.

_____

_____

WRITE ABOUT IT Compare "The Prince and the Tasty Pea" with "The Princess and the Pea." How are the two stories alike? How are they different?

_____

_____

_____

_____

_____

_____

_____

_____

_____

_____

_____

Prepare to Read

GENRE STUDY **Informational text** is nonfiction. It gives facts about a topic. As you read *Don't Touch Me!,* look for:

- captions with photos
- details and facts about a topic
- how visuals and words help you understand the text

SET A PURPOSE Read to find out the most important ideas in each part. Then **synthesize,** or put together these ideas in your mind, to find out what the text really means to you.

POWER WORDS

sharp

prickles

thorns

extra

poke

nasty

sensitive

attack

Build Background: Plant Predators

DON'T TOUCH ME!

by
Elizabeth Preston

Plants can't run away from hungry animals. So some of them fight back. They have defenses to keep creatures from eating them. These plants can scratch you or stab you. Some of them can make you sick. Others make you itch like crazy. Don't get too close, or you'll be sorry!

180

OW

Do you have a rose bush in your yard? Then you know these pretty flowers are better for sniffing than touching. Roses have sharp prickles on their stems. Some other plants, like the hawthorn, have woody thorns.

And beautiful holly leaves have very sharp points. (Holly leaves and berries have extra protection. They're poisonous!)

OW OW OW
OW OW OW

Cactus plants keep animals away with spines. Some cacti have arms—but hugging them is a bad idea.

Yowch!

A stinging nettle doesn't look as dangerous as a spiny cactus. But it's covered with sharp hairs called trichomes. The hairs are like tiny needles. If you touch them, they poke your skin with chemicals that sting and itch. You might get a nasty rash.

182

Itch

Poison ivy leaves have oils that can make you itchy. If your soccer ball rolls into a patch of poison ivy during a game, you might be scratching later. Poison oak and poison sumac are related plants that make the same oils. You can watch out for poison ivy by remembering the rhyme, "Leaves of three, let it be!"

Shy Plants

The sensitive or touch-me-not plant doesn't stab you, poison you, or make you itch. If you touch it, the plant quickly folds up its leaves.

Plants with Ants

Acacia trees have big, scary thorns. But for extra protection, they use ants. The ants have a special friendship with the tree. They live inside hollow thorns and eat food the tree makes for them. If a bug or a bigger animal comes too close, the ants attack and sting it.

Use details from *Don't Touch Me!* to answer these questions with a partner.

1. **Synthesize** How do plants protect themselves?

2. Why did the author write this text? What is she trying to persuade readers to do?

3. Compare *Don't Touch Me!* and *Experiment with What a Plant Needs to Grow*. How are the texts alike? What are the most important differences between them?

Talking Tip

Say your ideas. Speak clearly and not too fast or too slow.

I think that _____.

Write an Opinion

PROMPT In your opinion, which plant in *Don't Touch Me!* has the most extreme defenses? Look for details in the words and pictures to help you decide.

PLAN First, write which plant you chose in the chart. Then write or draw reasons why you chose that plant.

_____ has the most extreme defenses.

Reason	Reason	Reason

WRITE Now write your opinion about the plant you chose. Include reasons why you think that plant's defenses are the most extreme. Remember to:

- Use details from the words and photos.

- Use describing words.

_____

_____

_____

_____

_____

_____

_____

_____

_____

_____

_____

Prepare to Read

GENRE STUDY **Informational text** is nonfiction. It gives facts about a topic.

MAKE A PREDICTION Preview "Giant Pumpkin Races." Sometimes pumpkins grow to be very large! What do you think you will read about?

_____

_____

_____

_____

_____

_____

_____

SET A PURPOSE Read to find out how people grow giant pumpkins and have fun with them.

Giant Pumpkin Races

READ Which sentence tells the author's opinion? <u>Underline</u> it.

People do different things with pumpkins. They may draw silly faces on them or bake pumpkin pies. But the very silliest thing people do is hop inside them and race! That is just what happens at giant pumpkin races every fall.

It all begins with the pumpkin seeds. Farmers plant special seeds that will grow giant pumpkins. They make sure the seeds get enough sun, water, and fertilizer. ▶

Close Reading Tip

Mark important words with *.

CHECK MY UNDERSTANDING

What causes a pumpkin to grow to a very large size?

_____

_____

READ What is this part of the text mostly about?

Close Reading Tip

Mark ideas that support the author's opinion with *.

The fun begins at the giant pumpkin weigh-in. Farmers choose their biggest pumpkin. They weigh them on giant scales. The farmer whose pumpkin weighs the most wins prize money. The largest pumpkin on record was more than 2,500 pounds! That's almost equal to the weight of a small car!

Next, pumpkin paddlers have to scoop out those big pumpkins. The huge, hollow pumpkins are big enough to float even with a person inside them!

Soon, it's race time! Many racers wear funny costumes and decorate their pumpkin boats. Then, the race is on! May the best pumpkin win!

CHECK MY UNDERSTANDING

What makes giant pumpkin races fun?

_____

_____

_____

WRITE ABOUT IT How are the events in the text connected?
Use information from the selection to describe how the growth
of a pumpkin is connected to having fun at a pumpkin race.

_____

_____

_____

_____

_____

_____

_____

_____

_____

_____

_____

_____

Prepare to View

GENRE STUDY **Videos** are short movies that give you information or something for you to watch for enjoyment. As you watch *George Washington Carver: The Wizard of Tuskegee,* look for:

- how pictures, sounds, and words work together
- information about the topic
- the purpose of the video

SET A PURPOSE Ask yourself what happens and why to find **cause and effect** connections in the video. A cause is something that makes something else happen. An effect is what happens because of the cause.

Build Background: Made from Peanuts

GEORGE WASHINGTON CARVER

The Wizard of Tuskegee

by StoryBots

As You View Get to know George Washington Carver! Think about how puppets, rhyming words, and sound effects help to tell Mr. Carver's story in a fun way. Listen for details that tell what happened and why to help you understand how the events in his life are connected.

Use details from *George Washington Carver: The Wizard of Tuskegee* to answer these questions with a partner.

1. **Cause and Effect** What caused George Washington Carver to move to Tuskegee? What effect did that have on his work?

2. What did George do when he wasn't allowed to go to his neighborhood school? What does that tell you about him?

3. What does the narrator mean when he says that George "reached for the sky"?

Talking Tip

Add your own idea to your partner's. Be polite.

I like your idea. My idea is _____.

Let's Wrap Up!

(?) Essential Question

What do plants need to live and grow?

....

Pick one of these activities to show what you have learned about the topic.

1. Plant Instructions

You have read about what a plant needs to grow. Now, write instructions that tell someone how to grow a healthy plant. List the things he or she will need and the steps to follow. Draw pictures to go with each step in your instructions.

Word Challenge

Can you use the word survive in your instructions?

2. Grow a Poem

Work with a partner to write a poem about plants. Take turns writing one line for the poem and watch your poem grow. Be sure to include details you learned from the texts.

My Notes

Glossary

A

account [ə-kount′]   An account is a report of something that happened. My teacher gave an **account** of his trip.

achieve [ə-chēv′]   When you achieve something, you get it after a lot of hard work. You can **achieve** your goal if you work hard.

adorable [ə-dôr′ə-bəl]   Something adorable is cute and easy to love. That little lamb is **adorable**!

allowed [ə-loud′]   When you are allowed to do something, it is all right for you to do it. We are **allowed** to have a snack now.

alone [ə-lōn′]   When you do something alone, you do it by yourself. I went for a quiet walk **alone** on the trail.

approached [ə-prōcht′]   If someone approached you, that person got closer to you. The dog **approached** us slowly.

arrange [ə-rānj′]   If you arrange things, you put them in a certain order. Please **arrange** the boxes by size.

ashamed [ə-shāmd′]   When you are ashamed, you feel bad about something you have done. He was **ashamed** that he lost the money.

attack [ə-tăk′]   If you attack something, you try to hurt or damage it. The cat tried to **attack** a mouse.

C

communicate [kə-myōo′nĭ-kāt′]   When you communicate, you share information or ideas. Sign language is one way to **communicate**.

current [kûr′ənt, kŭr′ənt]   If something is current, it is happening in the present time. I have a **current** issue of the magazine.

198

D

dared [dârd]   If you dared to do something, you were brave enough to do it. We **dared** to jump into the cold water.

deal [dēl]   You deal with people by understanding and getting along with them. I know how to **deal** with a crying baby.

deserved [dĭ-zûrvd′]   If you deserved something, you earned it because of something you did. They **deserved** to take home the trophy.

E

elders [ĕl′dərz]   Elders are people who are older than you. She loved hearing stories from her **elders**.

extra [ĕk′strə]   An extra amount of something is more than usual. I took an **extra** glass of juice for my friend.

F

fertilize [fûr′tl-īz′]   When you fertilize soil, you add something that helps plants grow. **Fertilize** the soil before you plant seeds.

figured [fĭg′yərd]   If you figured out something, you came to understand it. Robbie **figured** out how to solve the problem.

fuels [fyōō′əlz]   Something that fuels another thing gives it power. Healthy food **fuels** the body.

G

germinate [jûr′mə-nāt′]   Seeds germinate when they begin to grow. The seeds began to **germinate** this week.

glanced [glănsd]   If you glanced at something, you looked at it quickly. I **glanced** at my watch while I walked.

H

hauling [hôl′ĭng]   When you are hauling something heavy, you are pulling it hard. We are **hauling** our wagon up the hill.

hurdle [hûr′dl]   A hurdle is a problem that could stop you from doing something.

Eliza leapt over each **hurdle** and was the first person to cross the finish line.

M

minerals [mĭn′ər-əlz]   Minerals are natural substances that do not come from plants or animals. The soil has **minerals** in it.

moisten [moi′sən]   When you moisten something, you wet it a little. **Moisten** a sponge before washing the dishes.

motioned [mō′shənd]   If you motioned, you moved your hand or head to show someone what to do. The museum guide **motioned** for us to follow her.

N

nasty [năs′tē]   When something is nasty, it is very unpleasant. I have a **nasty** scrape on my knee, but I will be ready to play by this weekend.

O

overflowing [ō′vər-flō′ĭng]   If something is overflowing, no more can fit in it. The glass was **overflowing** with water.

oversized [ō′vər-sīzd′]   Something oversized is very big. My father gave me an **oversized** shirt that I will grow into someday.

P

plenty [plĕn′tē]   When you have plenty, you have a lot of something. We have **plenty** of food for everyone.

poke [pōk]   If something jabs into you suddenly, it is said to poke you. Be careful not to **poke** yourself with the nails.

potential [pə-tĕn'shəl]   Potential is what you can do in the future if you work hard now. I have the **potential** to be a great swimmer.

prickles [prĭk'əlz]   Prickles are small points that stick out. The plant was covered with **prickles**.

pride [prīd]   When you feel pride, you are pleased about something you did well.

He spoke with **pride** about his work.

process [prŏs'ĕs', prō'sĕs']   A process is a series of steps that happen in order. Writing a book can be a long **process**.

provides [prə-vīdz']   Provides means to give something that is needed. The school **provides** pencils for students.

R

reminding [rĭ-mīnd'ĭng]   If you are reminding people, you are telling them again. This string on my finger is **reminding** me to water the garden.

S

secret [sē'krĭt]   When something is secret, very few people know about it. Kim had a funny **secret** to share.

seedlings [sēd'lĭngz]   Seedlings are young plants that grow from seeds. The **seedlings** are growing taller.

selfless [sĕlf'lĭs]   If you are selfless, you care more about others than yourself. My friend is **selfless** and likes to help others.

sensitive [sĕn'sĭ-tĭv]   If something is sensitive, it is quick to respond to something else. Some people are **sensitive** to the cold.

series [sîr'ēz]   A series is a group of things that come one after another. I read the whole **series** of books.

sharp [shärp]   If something is sharp, it has an edge that can cut you. This scissors were very **sharp**.

spiky [spī'kē]   Something spiky has sharp points. This tree has **spiky** leaves.

sprout [sprout]   When plants sprout, they begin to grow. The plant will **sprout** leaves.

starlit [stär'lĭt']   A starlit place gets its light from the stars. We took a walk under a pretty **starlit** sky.

statements [stāt'mənts]   Statements are words or sentences that people said or wrote to share information. I agree with your **statements** about being on time and working hard.

survive [sər-vīv']   When things survive, they stay alive. Animals and plants need water to **survive**.

swipe [swīp]   If you swipe something, you take it. I did not **swipe** your candy.

T

thorns [thôrnz]   Thorns are points that grow on a branch or stem. This plant has many **thorns**.

timeline [tīm'līn']   A timeline is a visual that shows events in the order they happened. This **timeline** tells us information about the history of communication.

W

whacked [wăkt, hwăkt]   If you whacked something, you hit it hard. Winston **whacked** the ball with all his might, and he got his very first home run.

whimpered [wĭm'pərd, hwĭm'pərd]   If you whimpered, you made a quiet, crying noise. The dog **whimpered** when it was home alone.

whir [wûr, hwûr]   A whir is a buzzing or humming sound. When we heard the **whir** of the mixer, we knew Mom was making us cookies.

Index of Titles and Authors

Acknowledgments

"Don't Touch Me!" by Elizabeth Preston from *CLICK* Magazine, October 2016. Text copyright © 2016 by Carus Publishing Company. Reprinted by permission of Cricket Media. All Cricket Media material is copyrighted by Carus Publishing d/b/a Cricket Media, and/or various authors and illustrators. Any commercial use or distribution of material without permission is strictly prohibited. Please visit http://www.cricketmedia.com/info/licensing for licensing and http://www.cricketmedia.com for subscriptions.

Drum Dream Girl (retitled from *Drum Dream Girl: How One Girl's Courage Changed Music*) by Margarita Engle, illustrated by Rafael López. Text copyright © 2015 by Margarita Engle. Illustrations copyright © 2015 by Rafael López. Reprinted by permission of Houghton Mifflin Harcourt Publishing Company.

Excerpt from *Experiment with What a Plant Needs to Grow* by Nadia Higgins. Text copyright © 2015 by Lerner Publishing Group, Inc. Reprinted with the permission of Lerner Publishing Company, a division of Lerner Publishing Group, Inc. All rights reserved. No part of this text excerpt may be used or reproduced in any manner whatsoever without the prior written permission of Lerner Publishing Group, Inc.

I Am Helen Keller by Brad Meltzer. Illustrated by Christopher Eliopoulos.

Text copyright © 2015 by Forty-four Steps, Inc. Illustrations copyright © 2015 by Christopher Eliopoulos. This edition published by arrangement and reprinted by permission of Dial Books for Young Readers, an imprint of Penguin Young Readers Group, a division of Penguin Random House, LLC and Writers House, LLC.

Excerpt from "Muhammad Ali: Don't Count Me Out" by Walter Leavy from EBONY® Magazine, March 1985. Text copyright © 1985 by EBONY Media Operations, LLC. Reprinted by permission of EBONY Media Operations, LLC.

Credits

4 (t) ©VaLiza/Shutterstock; 4 (c) ©DenisFilm/Shutterstock, (bg) ©BlurryMe/Shutterstock, (c) ©DenisFilm/Shutterstock, (b) ©Houghton Mifflin Harcourt; 5 (t) ©Eric Jenks; 5 (b) ©Transcendental Graphics/Getty Images Sport/Getty Images; 5 (b) ©Bettmann/Getty Images; 5 (b) ©Focus on Sport/Getty Images; 5 ©Transcendental Graphics/Getty Images Sport/Getty Images, ©STILLFX/Shutterstock, ©Bettmann/Getty Images, ©Focus on Sport/Getty Images, ©Billion Photos/Shutterstock; 6 ©cooperr/Shutterstock, ©Bohumil Taborik/Shutterstock; 6 (c) ©Cora Mueller/Shutterstock; 7 (c) ©Gwoeii/Shutterstock; 7 (c) ©magnetcreative/E+/Getty Images; 8 ©Flashpop/Stone/Getty Images; 12 ©VaLiza/Shutterstock; 13 (l) ©Agence France Presse/Hulton Archive/Getty Images; 13 (r) ©Hulton Archive/Stringer/Getty Images; 13 (bg) ©Houghton Mifflin Harcourt; 14 (bl) ©ThinkMoncur; 46 (bg) ©StockTrek/Photodisc/Getty Images; 47 (inset) ©NASA Still Photo Library; 48 ©NASA Kennedy Space Center; 50 (bg) ©Houghton Mifflin Harcourt; 50 (inset) ©hanohiki/iStock/Getty Images Plus; 50 (c) ©DenisFilm/Shutterstock, (bg) ©BlurryMe/Shutterstock, (c) ©DenisFilm/Shutterstock, (b) ©Houghton Mifflin Harcourt; 51 (r) ©Houghton Mifflin Harcourt; 52 (bl) ©FreeTransform/Getty Images; 52 (bc) ©North Wind Picture Archives/Alamy; 52 (br) ©Everett Historical/Shutterstock; 52 (tr) ©DenisFilm/Shutterstock; 52 (cr) ©Peshkova/Shutterstock; 52 (tl) ©LighteniR/Shutterstock; 52 (l) ©LighteniR/Shutterstock; 52 (l) ©LighteniR/Shutterstock; 52 (l) ©LighteniR/Shutterstock; 52 (l) ©LighteniR/Shutterstock; 52 (inset) ©Stefanie Finlayson/Houghton Mifflin Harcourt; 53 (l) ©Private Collection/Peter Newark American Pictures/ Bridgeman Images; 53 (c) ©Everett Collection Historical/Alamy; 53 (br) ©Library of Congress Prints & Photographs Division; 53 (tr) ©LighteniR/Shutterstock; 54 (bc) ©DenisFilm/Shutterstock; 54 (bl) ©dszc/E+/Getty Images; 54 (br) ©DNY59/iStock/Getty Images Plus; 54 (inset) ©Flashon Studio/Shutterstock; 54 (tl) ©DenisFilm/Shutterstock; 54 (c) ©Anatoly Tiplyashin/iStock; 54 (bg) ©Houghton Mifflin Harcourt; 54 (bg) ©Houghton Mifflin Harcourt; 54 (bg) ©Houghton Mifflin Harcourt; 54 (bg) ©BlurryMe/Shutterstock; 55 (br) ©DenisFilm/Shutterstock; 55 (bl) ©DenisFilm/Shutterstock; 55 (br) ©shank_ali/iStock/Getty Images Plus/Getty Images; 55 (bg) ©Houghton Mifflin Harcourt; 55 (bg) ©Houghton Mifflin Harcourt; 55 (bg) ©Houghton Mifflin Harcourt; 56 (t) ©Rova N/Shutterstock; 56 (tc) ©Rova N/Shutterstock; 56 (tc) ©Alfa Vector/